THE COLOSSEUM

PAST AND PRESENT

The Valley of the Colosseum
The Arch of Constantine
The Temple of Venus and Rome
Domus Aurea (Nero's Golden House)

LOZZI *Roma*
edizioni turistiche

GENERAL INDEX

THE COLOSSEUM

OPENING HOURS:
Daily 9 am - 4 pm (until 6 pm in Summer).
Wednesdays, Sundays and holidays 9 am - 1 pm.

ADMISSION:
Tickets cost 10,000 Lire, and can be purchased at the box offices at the entrances to the Colosseum, Roman Forum and Palatine.

© **1998 LOZZI ROMA s.a.s.**

Tutti i diritti sono riservati - riproduzione anche parziale vietata, sia a mezzo stampa che mediante supporti magnetici od elettronici.
No part of this book may be reproduced in whole or part or by any means in printed or electronic form without the express permission from the Publisher.

Direzione e redazione:
LOZZI ROMA sas
Via Filippo Nicolai, 91 - 00136 ROMA
Tel. 06 35497051 - Tel. e Fax 06 35497074
e-mail: lozzirm@spinweb.it

Stampato presso la tipografia PO.LI.GRAF srl
Via Vaccareccia, 41 b - Pomezia (Roma)

Fotolito TIPOCROM srl

Fotografie:
Archivio fotografico LOZZI ROMA s.a.s.
Le immagini alle pagine 8, 15, 21 (in basso), 31 sono state realizzate da S. Perretta.
La fotografia a pag. 32 è stata gentilmente offerta dalla Rolo Banca 1473.
I disegni alle pagine 14, 24, 25, sono tratti da *Fabbriche di Roma*, dell'arch. F. Turconi, Milano 1857. Il testo ci è stato messo cortesemente a disposizione da A. Busiri Vici.

THE COLOSSEUM IN NUMBERS

The Colosseum or Flavian Amphitheater, was built in just **5 years** of uninterrupted work between 75 a.D. and 80 a.D.

The external ellipse of the arena measures **188 by 156 meters**, and the complex occupies **3357 square meters**.

The façade of the Colosseum is **49 meters tall**, and divided into **three floors** with **80 arches** each, and surmounted by a windowed pilaster attic. 240 corbels correspond to holes in the attic which housed the shafts that supported the immense velarium (awning). With a surface area of 22,000 square meters, the velarium covered the arena at a height of about 50 meters. It was held by cords attached to a metal circle at the center, which had a circumference of 90 meters.

The **80 entrance arches** on the ground level were numbered, with the exception of the **four principal entran ces** with propylaeums, which were reserved for the emperor, the imperial family and the vestals. Spectators were given passes which indicated an assigned seat in a particular section, and even the route to that seat. Although entrance was free, seating depended on rigid social divisions.

The 17 rows of the podium were reserved for the imperial section, magistrates and senators. The low cavea was for the knights; the middle cavea, composed of **19 rows** and **32 entrances**, belonged to the middle class; the "Maenianum summum", or high cavea, formed by **37 rows**, was left to the general public. In total, there were **50 rows in stone**, while the sections for the plebes were built of wood. It is estimated that there was about **30,000 meters** of linear seating space - which would have accommodated **73,000 spectators**.

A great variety of **materials** were used to build the Colosseum: **travertine**, the calcareous stone from the area around Tivoli, to line the façade and for the concentric rings which supported the cavea; **tufa**, or soft volcanic rock, for the foundation and the radial walls; **concrete** to line the vaults of the galleries and arches; **marble** for the splendid finish, the capitals, the statues and the seats of the sections in the first rows; finally, an infinite number of **bricks** for non-structural walls and the screens.

HISTORY OF ANCIENT ROME

According to legend, Rome was founded in **753 BC**, when **Romulus**, its first king, traced a furrow in the earth to mark the boundaries of the city. Romulus was succeeded by six kings: The Sabine **Numa Pompilius** (715 BC - 673 BC); the Roman **Tullus Hostilius** (673 BC - 642 BC) under whom the city of Alba Longa was defeated; **Ancus Marcius** (641 BC - 617 BC); **Tarquinius Priscus** (616 BC - 579 BC), of Etruscan origin, like the Tarquins which followed, built projects like the Circus Maximus, the Cloaca Maxima and the Mammertine Prison; **Servius Tullius** (578 BC - 534 BC), contributed to the growth of the city through reforms of state institutions, the construction of an aqueduct and an imposing wall surrounding the city (the Servian Wall). The tyranny of the last king, **Tarquinius "the Superb"**, led the Roman people to overthrow the monarchy and establish the Roman Republic (509 BC).

The urban growth of Rome under the monarchy was accompanied by a notable increase in the population, which by 500 BC had reached nearly 15,000 for the 100 square-kilometer area. Rome had by then become an important political center, adorned by public works of notable artistic value; the Forum was paved and the Temple of Jupiter rose on the Capital Hill.

Marcus Tullus Cicero (1st century AD), great Latin writer and orator. Rome, Capitoline Museums.

Under the monarchy the social order had been based on the clear division of classes between the aristocracy of the patricians, descendants of the oldest Roman families, and the rest of the population, the plebes, who were excluded from political life. The state was ruled by the king, the senate, the curia and its committees. With the advent of the **Republic**, the Senate elected two consuls (instead of a king) to lead Rome. The praetors administered justice and the questors managed the treasury.

On the military front, the young Republic immediately had to confront threats from the Etruscans and went to war against the Latin League, which did not tolerate Roman territorial supremacy. But already by the end of the 6th century BC, Rome dominated Lazio and the area south of the Tiber.

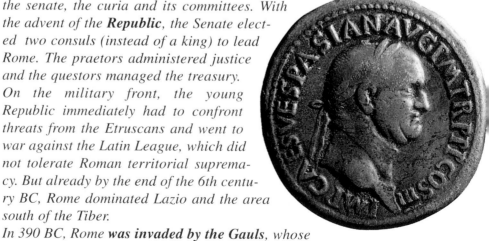

Bronze coin with the profile of the Emperor Vespasian (70 AD).

In 390 BC, Rome **was invaded by the Gauls**, whose victory favored the rise, however short-lived, of other Italic peoples. The mid-4th century BC saw a large Roman expansion into Central-Southern Italy. When the Romans took control of the Magnagrecia (further south), they could no longer ignore the Mediterranean power of Carthage.

In 264 BC, under the pretext of the control of Eastern Sicily, Rome and Carthage fought what was to be the **First Punic War**. A strong Roman navy ensured victory in 241 BC. With the peace treaty Rome annexed Sicily, and later Sardinia and Corsica.

In 222 BC, the Roman legions put an end to the incursions of the Gauls and Ligurians, which had begun six years earlier. This military success greatly enlarged the Roman territory into the Po valley.

In 218 BC **Hannibal** led the Carthaginian armies to Italy through Spain, crossing the Pyranees and the Alps and winning important victories all along the peninsula. Though Rome was left without defense, a campaign in Africa conducted by the Roman general **Scipio "Africanus"** forced Hannibal's armies to halt their advance on Rome, withdraw and return to Carthage, where they were ultimately defeated in 202 BC.

With an enlarged territory and sphere of influence, Rome found itself in competition with ever more dangerous adversaries. The rich and advanced east, the cradle of the classical world, became a new theater of battle: In 200 BC, Rome went to war with Phillip of Macedon and in 191 BC with Antiochus of Syria. Greece was made part of Rome in 146 BC. In the same year the Senate ordered the legions to destroy the Carthaginians once and for all.

A fierce war broke out in 90 BC on the Italian peninsula between Romans and the other Italic peoples, who had been attempting for years to get the rights enjoyed by Roman citizens. Before the Roman legions won the war in 88 BC, the Senate gave in and agreed to extend the rights of citizenship. In the meantime, the insurrection of the Asian provinces and the war against Mithridate, king of Ponto, brought about the rise of the autocrat **Sulla**.

His victory in Asia allowed him, once he returned to Italy, to violently oppose the power of the democrats led by **Marius and Cinna**, against whom he started a bloody civil war. After victory in 82 BC, Sulla had the Senate nominate him as dictator-for-life to restore the oligarchy of the Republic.

In 71 BC, **Pompey** and **Crassus** were elected as consuls and diminished the role of the Senate in favor of the tribunes

Bust of the Emperor Trajan (98-117 AD). Rome, Capitoline Museums.

Gold coin with the profile of the Emperor Octavian Augustus (2 AD).

and the knights. It was this conflict between the popular party (represented by Pompey and Crassus) and the Senate which prompted an accord between the two consuls and **Caius Julius Caesar**, a young aristocrat.

The election of Caesar as Consul in 59 BC solidified this alliance - the first Triumvirate. Caesar continued the policies of his allies and began a campaign in Gaul which ended in victory in 51 BC, after his consular mandate had ended. Pompey and Crassus had in the meantime again been elected as Consuls, but with Crassus' death in Syria and Pompey's gradual shift toward conservatives in the Senate, a break emerged between the two ex-triumvirs.

This intensified when Julius Caesar was formally invited by the Senate and by Pompey to disband his legions. Caesar's refusal to do so began a terrible civil war that forced the escape of Pompey and many senators to the Balkans, where they were defeated at the **battle of Farsalo** in Thessaly (48 BC).

Returning to Rome without rivals, Caesar was nominated Consul in 48 BC and dictator-for-life four years later. But the sum of power acquired by this single man aroused the resentment and political hostility of his former allies. In March of 44 BC, a plot hatched in the Senate and led by **Brutus** and **Cassius** put an end to the life and ambitions of Julius Caesar.

The attempts to restore the Republic in 43 BC were blocked by an alliance between **Marc Antony**, **Lepidus** and **Octavian** (great nephew and adopted son of Caesar, thus nominated Consul by the Senate). The second triumvirate attempted to write a new constitution, and decisively defeated the Republicans Brutus and Cassius at the battle of Filippi in 42 BC. But the cohesion of the triumvirate soon weakened in the absence of a common enemy. The antagonism between Octavian and Antony crushed Lepidus, who soon withdrew, and Octavian secured victory in 31 BC at the **battle of Actium**.

The crisis of the Republic, which had started in the time of the Gracchi, ended with the "**golden age**" of **Octavian Augustus**.

Octavian initiated a long period of peace and political stability, creating the foundation for a new order upon which **imperial Rome** was to be built. The Senate was retained in deference to the traditions of the Roman aristocracy; the essential novelty was the figure of the *prince*, who at the vortex of the state oversaw and coordinated the institutions.

After eight uninterrupted years as consul and numerous symbolic tributes, in 27 BC Octavian Augustus had himself assigned the title of **Emperor**, with which he assumed an unlimited power over the armies and the provinces. In 12 BC he was honored with the title of

Marble bust of the Emperor Nero (54-68 AD). Rome, Capitoline Museums.

Gold coin with the profile of the Emperor Nero.

Pontifex Maximus *(Highest Priest)*.

Virgil, *Horace*, *Ovid* and *Livy* were the most meaningful poetic and literary exponents of the Augustean age, which can be considered among the most exciting periods in Roman history. On the artistic and urban level, it was the era in which the Empire learned to celebrate itself. The triumphal arches, the grandiose monuments, and the ever more marvelous Imperial Fora exalted the greatness of Rome and its emperors.

At the death of Augustus in 14 AD, the fundamental lines had been drawn and the imperial regime went on for two strong and vital centuries. The differences between Italy and the provinces were reduced and Roman citizenship was progressively extended as the aristocracy and the "bourgeoisie" of the provinces were integrated into the ruling class of the Empire.

The legacy of Octavian was passed to his adopted son **Tiberius** *who continued the* **Julian dynasty**. **Caligula** *followed from 37 AD to 41 AD;* **Claudius** *from 41 AD to 54 AD, who was succeeded by the young* **Nero**, *whose reign was marked by a policy of terror which was so unpopular that he was deposed by the Senate in 68 AD and declared an outlaw.*

*Between 68 AD and 69 AD the armies in the provinces elected three emperors (**Galba**, **Otho** and **Vitellius**), who killed one another. In 69 AD **Flavius Vespasian**, who had suppressed the revolts in Palestine, began the **Flavian dynasty**, which restored order and reinforced the boundaries of the Empire. He was succeeded by his two sons, **Titus** in 79 AD and immediately after by **Domitian** in 81 AD, who surrounded himself with an imposing military force and ruled so tyrannically that he was killed in a palace plot in 96 AD.*

*The Senate then managed to bring the power of the Empire to one of its own, **Nerva**. This began the period during which the emperor, together with the Senate, selected the imperial successor based on considerations of political order and morale, rather than dynasty or bloodlines. This was one of the happiest times in the history of Rome, with long periods of peace and great military successes in the east, Eastern Europe, and in the north, which marked the* pax romana *in the known world.*

During the first and second centuries, after the disastrous fire that engulfed Rome during the reign of Nero, there was urban development on a grand scale.

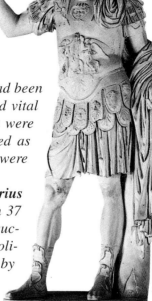

Statue of the Emperor Marcus Aurelius (2nd century AD). Rome, Capitoline Museums.

Emperor Septimius Severus (192-211 AD), bust in marble and alabaster. Rome, Capitoline Museums.

(see page 10)

A Roman mosaic (late-Imperial period), with fighting gladiators. Their names, *Astyanax* and *Kalendio*, are clearly written above. Gladiators fought with distinctly different weapons and styles of combat (among them *retarii, oplomachi, secutores, provocatores* and *traces*), so much so that the crowds in the Colosseum took sides, rooting enthusiastically for one over the other.

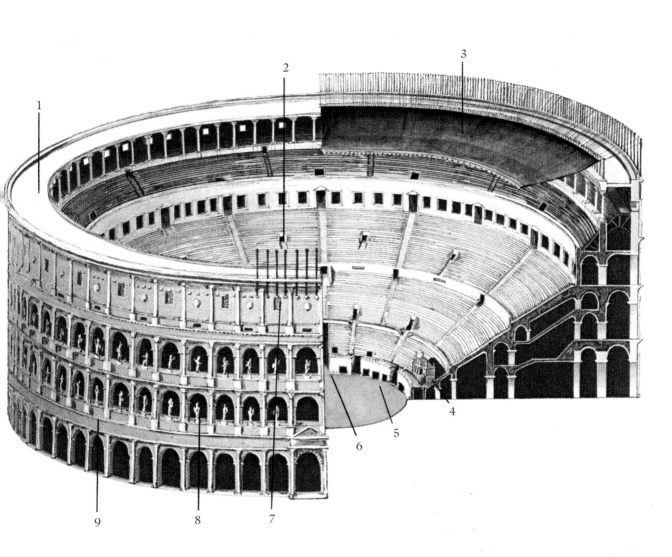

1. *From the top of the amphitheater, 80 sailors from the Imperial fleet worked the enormous* velarium *that covered the cavea during the games.*

2. *Numbered entrances allowed the tens of thousands of spectators to flow easily in and out of the Colosseum.*

3. *The* velarium. *Its extension and tensioning lasted four days.*

4. *Imperial Tribune.*

5. *Entrances for the animals.*

6. *Entrance for the gladiators.*

7. *240 supporting shafts were necessary to support the velarium and its cords.*

8. *Statues of gods. Each arch housed a different statue.*

9. *The façade, with three orders of arches, were covered in Travertine extracted from caves at Tivoli.*

Under the Flavian emperors, the Colosseum, the Baths of Titus, the Palace of Domitian and the Stadium of Domitian (now Piazza Navona) were built. Just before his death in 98 AD, Nerva chose the Spanish-born **Trajan**, an able general and much admired leader, as his successor.

In his nineteen year reign, Trajan devoted his energy principally to military campaigns, conquering Dacia (modern-day Romania), Mesopotamia and Arabia, thereby bringing the Empire to its largest extent ever. Such a policy was not followed by the eclectic **Hadrian**, adopted by Trajan and emperor from 117 AD to 138 AD, who pursued a peaceful policy of maintaining the borders, and dedicated himself to the arts, Hellenistic culture and long travels in the provinces.

Antonius Pius (138 AD - 161 AD) and **Marcus Aurelius** (161 AD - 180 AD) succeeded Hadrian. The latter, who was born in Africa, put an end to succession by adoption when he selected his son **Commodus** (180 AD - 192 AD), who had participated in the government since 176 AD, as his successor.

The successor **Septimius Severus**, a brave military commander, centralized the military administration and concerned himself with defending the borders of the Empire from the ever more present barbarian threat. In 211 AD, he was succeeded by his son **Caracalla**, who the following year proclaimed the Antoninian Law, extending the rights of citizenship to all people living within the borders of the Empire. The Servian dynasty was interrupted by the death of **Alexander Severus**.

Worried about the possibility of barbarian attack, **Aurelian** had an imposing wall built (270 AD - 275 AD) around the city, much of which is still visible. At the end of the 3rd century, **Diocletian** (280 AD - 305 AD) tried to re-establish centralized power and institutionalized the imperial theocracy by which a religious significance was attributed to the emperor. By then there were many Christians and this aggravated their opposition to the Empire and its repressive nature. The battles that followed the abdication of Diocletian were brought to an end only with the victory of **Constantine** over his rival **Maxentius** in 312 AD. One year later, with the Edict of Milan, the new emperor recognized Christianity, which then became the dominant religion of the Empire.

The most important act of the final years of Constantine's reign, which ended with his death in 337 AD, was the transfer of the imperial capital to Byzantium, on the Straits of the Dardanelles. Enlarged and embellished with splendid monuments, the city took the name Constantinople in 330 AD. This epochal shift caused by geopolitical events led to a rapid transformation of the very essence of the Roman Empire.

The Emperor Caracalla (early 3rd century AD). Paris, The Louvre.

Portrait of Heliogabalus (3rd century AD). Rome, Capitoline Museums.

The Colosseum in 1840, painted by Ippolito Caffi (1809-1866).

THE VALLEY OF THE COLOSSEUM

Roman chariot. Rome, Museum of
Roman Civilization.

The Valley of the Colosseum. Aerial view.

The very word **Colosseum** evokes the indelible image of
one of the world's most famous monuments.

After re-routing traffic in the early 1980's, several important excavations were carried out in the piazza at the foot
of the imposing structure, bringing to light precious infor-
mation about the area before the construction of the
amphitheater.

Above all, the remains date to the era of Nero. The
Colosseum was begun just eleven years after the death of
the emperor, who had built an artificial lake and a small
dock on the site. Surrounding it were buildings of rather
fanciful design, which completed the spectacular park of
the **Domus Aurea** (Nero's Golden House).

The excavations also revealed a simple but imposing fountain, the **Meta Sudans**, in the form of a very tall cone that
looked like the *meta* (turning post) from the circus. Instead
of a vertical spurt, which would have been dwarfed by the

greatness of the Colosseum nearby, a veil of water "sweated" from the fountain. The Meta had particular importance as the intersection of the three regions of Rome, the Celian, Palatine and Esquiline Hills, and as many primary roads. The remains of the Meta Sudans were visible until the 1930's, when the ancient fountain and the remains of an even more celebrated monument, the *Colossus of Nero*, were summarily removed so as not to impede the military parades and demonstrations along Via dell'Impero (today called Via dei Fori Imperiali) to consecrate the "romanità" (roman-ness) of the Fascist regime.

The 35 meter high Colossus of Nero first stood in the atrium of the Domus Aurea (Golden House), and was later moved near the Colosseum. Today, there are only the remains of the square perimeter of the base of the enormous statue, from which the Flavian Amphitheater took the name "Colosseum."

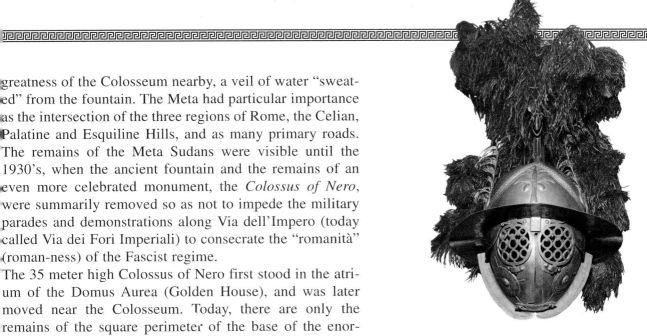

Helmet used by gladiators.
Rome, Museum of Roman Civilization.

The Valley of the Colosseum, in a model of Imperial Rome. Rome, Museum of Roman Civilization.

THE ARCH OF CONSTANTINE

A capital of the Arch of Constantine.

The area of the excavations reaches the shelter of the *Arch of Constantine*, the most grandiose of the three surviving triumphal arches. It was built in 315 AD in honor of the victory of Constantine over his rival Maxentius (312 AD), and also the incipient triumph of Christianity, by way of an allusion to an abstract "divinity" in place of the usual gods from pagan Olympus. At a height of 25 meters, the arch is the largest in Rome.

It is made up of pieces from different eras, ranging from the 1st century AD (columns, architraves, part of the attic) to the early years of the 4th century AD, when the two medallions on the short sides, the freezes on the side arches (among them the scene of the battle of the Milvian Bridge) and the bases of the columns were sculpted - the only portions made for the arch.

In fact, Rome's loss of a central political role in the Empire, which had by then impoverished the city, led to the gradual disappearance of important marble workshops, which in preceding centuries had prospered with the continual celebration of the greatness of Rome in monuments. This explained the need to reuse entire portions of pre-existing monuments which belonged to the era of Trajan, Hadrian and Commodus.

The Arch of Constantine.

The Arch of Constantine by night.

THE TEMPLE OF VENUS AND ROME

The Temple of Venus and Rome as seen through an arch of the Colosseum.

Reconstruction of the Temple of Venus and Rome.

The enormous podium that extended between the Basilica of Maxentius and the Piazza of the Colosseum belonged to the *Temple of Venus and Rome*, built in honor of the two goddesses and probably designed by Hadrian in 135 AD. Legend has it that the emperor asked the famous architect Apollodorus of Damascus, already ostracized by Hadrian, for his opinion of the then partially built temple. The architect's frank response explaining the various defects in the design so enraged the emperor that he had the architect put to death.

The Hellenistic-style twin temples with horizontally- opposed cellae was conceived by Hadrian. Such a design highlighted the reciprocal relationship between the goddesses Rome and Venus, progenitors of the city and the Empire. In order to make room for the temple, Hadrian had the Colossus of Nero removed from the vestibule of the Domus Aurea.

It was the greatest temple in Rome. The part dedicated to Venus extended toward the Colosseum, and was supported by a high platform which is still visible, as is the pavement of the cellae and the apse. The diamond-shaped coffers which decorate the apse date to a restoration by Maxentius after a fire destroyed the temple in 307 AD; they are identical to those in the nearby Basilica of Maxentius.

THE COLOSSEUM

Built by the emperors of the Flavian family on the area which had been the nymphaeum of Nero's Domus Aurea, the *Colosseum* was originally called the *Flavian Amphiteater*. It was designed as a free venue for the games, and celebrated the generous restitution to the Roman people of the vast tract of public land which Nero had taken to build his immense Golden House. The Roman people appreciated this gift from Vespasian and his sons Titus and Domitian, especially because up until then, there had not been a permanent venue for the gladiatorial games, the form of public sport which the Romans had preferred for centuries. Enormous problems due to the marsh-like nature of the land were resolved with a technology analogous to modern reinforced cement, and construction was completed with incredible speed, thanks to the simultaneous work of four workshops in the four quarters that made up the structure. Materials included brick, soft volcanic rock, 100,000 cubic meters of travertine (the transportation of which was made possible by a special road built between the site and the mines in Tivoli) and 300 tons of iron for the braces, many of which were taken in the centuries of decay, leaving the holes that are evident today.

The historian Suetonius, in his "Life of Titus", tells of the one hundred days of sumptuous celebrations that inaugurated the Colosseum in 80 AD, which were attended by all the important men of the Roman world, from every province of the Empire. The inauguration was also commemorated by a new bronze sesterce coin, which the Senate stamped in honor of the Emperor Titus. On the other side of the coin was the amphitheater packed with crowds. The preferred games were the *venationes*, or hunts, the gladiator duels and small naval battles; at the intermission there were various performances, singers, dancers, and the exposition of rare animals.

No historian recorded the killing of Christians, though undoubtedly between the cruel games that took place and frequent public executions of those condemned to death, there were many Christians killed here. The new religion, however, spread ever more, and left a sign of its growing influence in the 4th century AD: not only the emperors connected to Christianity like Constantine and Onorius, but also Julian, who restored paganism, issued edicts to bring an end to games with human victims.

Yet these cruel shows continued for more than a century; the last on record dates to 523 AD, when the Barbarian king

The Colosseum. The buttress was built by the architect Giuseppe Valadier in 1827.

Reconstruction of a section of the Colosseum.

Reconstruction of the exterior of the Colosseum.
Rome, Museum of Roman Civilization.

Gladiatorial combat in the arena of the Colosseum.

Theodoric agreed with the designated consul to permit a hunt for animals.

In the middle ages Rome's population fell to a few tens of thousands and several earthquakes and fires contributed considerably to the deterioration of the monument, which, in the 6th century, was even used as a cemetery. Still, back in the 8th century, the Venerable Bede, coming to Rome from England, proclaimed that "as long as the Colosseum stands, Rome will stand; when Rome falls, so shall the world."

In the following centuries, when the most powerful Roman families fought one another for control of the city and papacy, the Colosseum was transformed into a fortress by the powerful Frangipane and Savelli families, and in this way protected from further damage.

Ironically, it was in the Renaissance, the period with the greatest passion for antiquity, that the destruction of the Colosseum and the Roman Forum really began. The renewed building activity led the builders of some of Rome's most important buildings, such as Palazzo Venezia and St. Peter's, to use this unique monument as a mine for marble and construction materials, many of which sat abandoned on the ground after collapse caused by periodic earthquakes.

The fundamental work by the great 19th century archaeolo-

gist Rodolfo Lanciani, "The Destruction of Ancient Rome", disproved the common notion that held that the destruction and in many cases the disappearance of monuments of ancient Rome was due to the barbarian invasions, and later to the sacks of the Saracens, Normans, and Lansquenets. Instead it was the Romans themselves who had turned the Colosseum into a mine for precious materials with which they built new buildings.

There were also several unusual ideas about what to do with the aged structure, such as that of Pope Sixtus V, who wanted to turn it into a wool mill. The havoc ended in the 18th century, when Pope Benedict XIV, in the spirit of the newly discovered science of archaeology, restored the monument and at the same time consecrated it as position on the Via Crucis (Road of the Cross), which was subsequently moved.

Despite another restoration by the neoclassical architect Giuseppe Valadier, the romantic beauty of the richly overgrown ruin seduced writers such as Dickens and Stendhal. Only scientific excavations carried out at the end of the 19th and the beginning of the 20th century left the Colosseum as it looks today.

The dangers posed by smog, traffic and the uninterrupted flow of visitors highlights the need for ever more sophisticat-

The Flavian Amphitheater, commonly known as the Colosseum.

Gladiators facing one another in mortal combat, as shown in a 3rd century AD Roman mosaic. Rome, Museo Borghese.

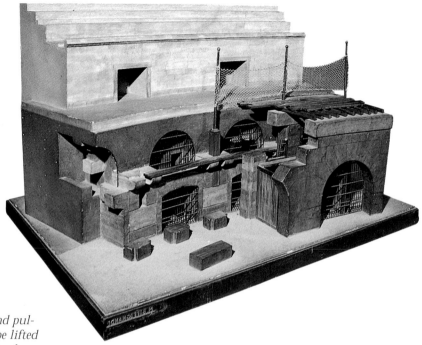

A complex system of weights and pulleys allowed the wild beasts to be lifted from their cages to the arena level.

Underground passageways of the Colosseum.

ed and rigorous means to protect and maintain the integrity of this splendid historical legacy, which in every part of the world is identified with the majesty of ancient Rome.

The exterior of the Colosseum, even if stripped, mutilated (only half of the structure remains intact) and supported by two buttresses, still preserves all of the distinct beauty of its original design. In compact, rhythmic succession, the most significant motif of Roman architecture is exalted here: the union of the arch and the architrave. Graceful variety in such solid unity emanates from the succession of the three classic orders in the capitals of the half-columns that separate the arches: the solid Doric of the ground floor, the elegant Ionic of the first floor, and the capricious Corinthian of the second floor, repeated in the pilaster strips of the smooth surface of the attic which seal everything together.

The Colosseum is a true masterpiece of engineering, not only for its solidity and functionality, but also for its resistance to the ravages of time. The dimensions of the monument are eloquent: the elliptical plan measures 188 meters at its greater axis, 156 in its shorter axis, and reached a height of about 50 meters. According to documentary evidence and complex calculations, it accommodated between seventy and eighty thousand spectators.

A series of corbels in the attic are coupled with holes, into which inserted the ingenious system of intersecting poles which supported the enormous *velarium* (awning) which protected the interior of the Colosseum from the elements. It had a surface area of 22,000 square meters and was made of silk and linen.

The complex maneuvers to control the awning were performed by a squad of sailors from the military port of Capo Miseno. They lived in one of the numerous barracks nearby, closely connected to the activities of the amphitheater (among other things, the barracks included an armory, a hospital and a morgue, where the bodies of gladiators killed in bloody duels were undressed).

The system of public access was extremely efficient: the 80 external arches were numbered (some of the numbers are still visible today), and spectators had passes which corresponded to a particular numbered entrance.

The four unnumbered arches which correspond to the four principal axes of the ellipse were reserved for the emperor, dignitaries and the vestals. The entrance of honor, on the north side, was protected by a portico decorated with stems and frescoes and led directly to the imperial tribune (*pulvinar*).

The Colosseum. The interior, visited by a cat.

Ground level passageways of the Colosseum.

Though much different than it was originally, the interior is still striking nonetheless, and the beauty of this majestic structure cannot easily be disassociated fron the horror of blood spilled here to furnish the Romans with the spectacle which they enjoyed most. The monument, however, does not seem to bear the slightest memory of so much violence. Instead, it rises here before us with the vibrant, humbling force of its stones, all the more admirable for its truly modern functionality, grandiose scale and the beauty of its architectural ingenuity. The richness of the decorations was provided for down to every particular. Literary sources describe vaults painted in gold and purple, walls which abounded with mosaics, numerous fountains flowing with perfumed water, awnings and cushions of precious materials (in the patrician sections).

The arena was made up of a movable wooden floor, covered in sand, which was cleaned and raked after every event. The surrounding seating area was separated from the arena by a retaining wall and a strong protective net topped with several elephant tusks to provide extra protection.

The area underneath was divided into galleries which were used as passageways and storage space for any materials necessary for the events in the arena above, including weapons,

Marble relief of Marcus Aurelius on horseback, receiving the defeated barbarians (180 d.C). Rome, Capitoline Museums.

Reconstruction of the interior of the Colosseum.

wild beasts, and scenery such as temples, hills, and forests. A system of lifts and counterweights served to raise scenery, animals and participants to the arena level. The dramatic appearance of the combatants would arouse an enthusiastic welcome from the spectators in the stands.

The poet Martial tells of an event with a realistic forest scene, with rocks and various animals, in which a man condemned to death interpreted the mythological character of Orpheus, and was actually torn to pieces by a bear.

Very little remains of the **seating areas**, which were divided into five sections. The first was reserved for the Senate and had marble stands; the successive sections were finished in brick, while the last section, reserved for common women, was finished in wood. The public was rigorously divided according to social class, as demonstrated by the remains of several inscriptions in the few remaining rows.

At the extreme of the major axis were two stands, one for the emperor, the other for the magistrates, vestals and others. The highly organized positioning of passageways and stairways in the four sections of stands, which were accessed from corresponding entrances, allowed the tens of thousands of spectators to fill and empty the Colosseum very quickly.

Marble relief of an Imperial chariot.
Rome, Capitoline Museums.

The interior of the Colosseum

Drawing of the north-east façade of the Arch of Constantine. Below, the two sides of the Arch.

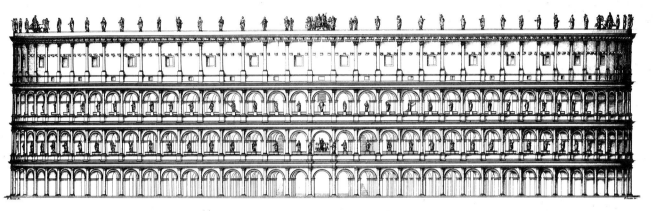

Detailed reconstruction of the exterior of the Colosseum.

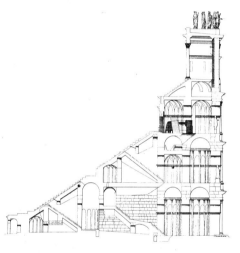

Drawing of a reconstruction of a section-view of the Colosseum.

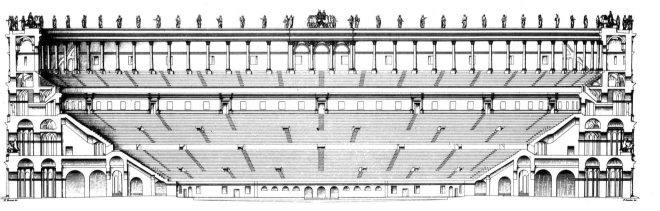

Detailed reconstruction of the interior of the Colosseum.

Faithful reconstruction of the Flavian Amphitheater, from a model by the architect Arturo Gismondi. Rome, Museum of Roman Civilization.

Aerial view of the Colosseum. On the left, the Arch of Constantine.

THE GAMES IN THE FLAVIAN AMPHITHEATRE

*T*he public spectacles of ancient Rome were generically called ludi. They were organized for festive occasions, celebrations and official anniversaries (ludi stati) thanks to the generous sponsorship of public figures or particularly wealthy private citizens.

The organizer of the games, the editor, *took care of the recruitment and payment of the gladiators, selecting them from those condemned to death, slaves, prisoners of war, and the free men who had decided to fight in the arena for the money and glory.*

There were essentially three types of games: ludi scaenici, *based on theatrical shows;* ludi circenses, *spectacles that could vary from the* naumachie *(battles between small scale boats) to* venationes, *actual hunting games; and finally the* munera, *gruesome duels between gladiators.*

The Colosseum was built to host both the ludi circenses and munera. By the 1st century AD, imperial Rome needed a stadium for the ludi circenses, with an extraordinary capacity to welcome a public increasingly passionate and numerous. Furthermore, the magnificence of the spectacles required a structure sufficient to support ever more elaborate scenery.

The sudden appearance of animals in the arena, perhaps while gladiators were dueling to the death, or the use of true special effects to render the scenery ever more realistic, won the support and passion of the public, who saluted with excitement and ovations the successive and ever more brilliantly innovative scenery.

The venationes were held in an arena at times transformed into a natural habitat for ferocious animals brought from the most remote zones of the Empire.

Spectators often placed wagers on battles between many different animals. Public execution of those condemned ad bestias (to be devoured by wild animals, such as lions, tigers and bears) thrilled the public taste for particularly blood-curdling spectacles. It seems that the Christians, who were considered to pose a danger to the integrity of the Empire, did not escape such a fate.

The passion for the violent spectacles found its greatest expression in the munera, instituted in 105 AD by the state. These games were rooted in the ancient traditions of the region; after the death of a relative, the wealthiest families organized ritual celebrations which culminated in public duels.

Already in the Republican era, therefore before the construction of the Colosseum, gladiatorial combat had been held before ever growing crowds, so much so that candidates for public office began to offer voters games that were ever more engaging and atrocious, in hope of winning fame and gratitude. Almost every emperor used the promise of extraordinary munera as a useful instrument to win popular consensus.

In the Colosseum, more than in anywhere else, bets multiplied when gladiators fought to the death, thus increasing the virulence of the fans. More than 73,000 frenzied Romans of every social class wildly cheered their favorites, often chosen on the basis of the type of weapon or style of combat used.

In these situations, even the most important citizens would sometimes go down to the arena to fight and plunge into the general euphoria. It is said the emperor Commodus

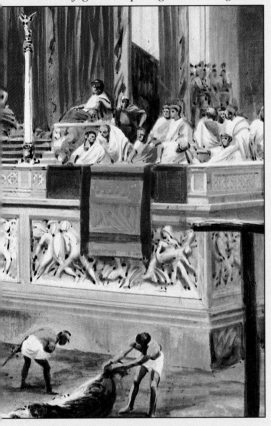

enjoyed going against the bears and killed one hundred of them in a single day. As for the Roman women, they were all entranced by the ardor and physical beauty of the gladiators, who battled semi-nude, greased with oil and strewn with sand.

The combat often concluded with the death of one of the combatants, but if one was disarmed or injured so as not to be able to defend himself, he had to prostrate himself before his adversary, raise his right hand and plead for mercy. The winner turned toward the emperor who, after consulting the people, gave his response with his thumb: extended upwards for mercy or turned down for death.

In the sportulae, introduced by the Emperor Claudius, many duels were held at the same time, creating a great massacre which lasted from sunrise to sunset and sometimes for many days on end.

The inauguration of the Colosseum, in 80 AD, was celebrated with one hundred consecutive days of carousing and carnage, which included the killing of 5000 animals and the death of 100 gladiators. In 109, under Trajan, an uninterrupted munera was held between July and November, in which about 10,000 gladiators perished. The celebration in 249 AD of the millenary anniversary of the founding of Rome was celebrated in the Colosseum with dozens of spectacles, among which a battle that included a thousand pairs of gladiators fighting simultaneously, while surrounded by cruel battles against ferocious animals of every kind. Historical sources note that for these celebrations 200 gladiators were killed, along with 60 lions, 40 wild horses, 32 elephants, 10 tigers, 6 hippopotamus, and 10 hyenas. The last violent show took place in 1332, when 18 knights and 11 bulls were killed in the Colosseum.

The Arch of Constantine.

The Flavian Amphitheater as seen from the Oppian Hill..

NERO'S GOLDEN HOUSE

The ruins of the *Domus Aurea* (Golden House) are up a short road that leads to the southeast side of the Colosseum. They are the half-buried remains of one of the most mysterious and fascinating buildings of ancient Rome, the splendid residence that Nero feverishly built in the few years between the great fire of 64 AD and his tragic death in 69 AD.

The Golden House was actually a spectacular complex of pavilions sparkling with gold, ivory, precious stone and polychromatic marble, immersed in a green countryside artificially constructed inside the city.

The perimeter of the fairy-like park extended from the Velia to the Oppian Hill, including all of the area where the Colosseum stands. Of the many marvels, however, almost all disappeared right after the death of Nero: successive emperors did all they could to erase even the memory of this undertaking.

Even the central pavilion, which served as the actual imperial residence, was completely covered by the baths built on the site by Trajan; in 104 AD, after a terrible fire, he had the ruins

of the upper floor leveled and filled in a good portion of the floor below, thus creating a solid base for the new building. For many centuries the Domus Aurea seemed lost; only in 1500 was its existence rediscovered as artists of the Renaissance lowered themselves with rope into the dark and gloomy grottoes to see the delicate pictorial decorations, which were from then on called "grotesques".

Night view of the two orders of arches of the Colosseum.

The Colosseum. Aerial view.

MAP OF THE FORUMS, PALATINE AND COLOSSEUM
PIANTA DEI FORI, DEL PALATINO E DEL COLOSSEO

english

ROMAN FORUM: 1 Basilica Emilia - 2 The Curia - 3 Church of the Saints Luke and Martine - 4 Lapis Niger - 5 Arch of Septimius Severus - 6 The Rostra - 7 Tabularium - 8 Portico of the Dei Consenti - 9 Temple of Vespasian 10 Temple of Saturn - 11 Column of Phoca - 12 Basilica Julia - 13 Temple of Castor and Pollux - 14 Temple of God Julius Caesar - 15 Church of St. Maria Antiqua - 16 Temple of Vesta - 17 House of Vestal Virgins - 18 The Regia - 19 Temple of Antoninus and Faustina - 20 Church of St. Lorenzo in Miranda - 21 Circular Temple of Romulus - 22 Basilica of Maxentius - 23 Antiquarium of the Forum - 24 Church of St. Francesca Romana - 25 Temple of Venus and Rome - 26 Arch of Titus.

THE PALATINE: 27 The Farnesian vegetable-gardens - 28 House of Livia - 29 House of Augustus - 30 Temple of Apollo - 31 Domus Tiberiana (House of Tiberius) - 32 Museum of Palatine - 33 Palace of the Flavii - 34 Domus Augustana - 35 Stadium of Domitian.

IMPERIAL FORUMS: 36 Forum of Julius Caesar - 37 Forum of Trajan - 38 Column of Trajan - 39 Trajan's Markets - 40 Forum of Augustus - 41 Temple of Mars Ultor - 42 Forum of Nerva - 43 Forum of Vespasian - 44 Marble maps of the Roman Empire.

THE COLOSSEUM VALLEY: 45 The Colosseum or Flavian Amphitheatre - 46 Arch of Constantine - 47 Meta Sudans - 48 Domus Aurea.

italiano

FORO ROMANO: 1 Basilica Emilia - 2 Curia - 3 Chiesa dei Santi Martina e Luca - 4 Lapis Niger - 5 Arco di Settimio Severo - 6 I Rostri - 7 - Tabularium - 8 Portico degli Dei Consenti - 9 Tempio di Vespasiano - 10 Tempio di Saturno - 11 Colonna di Foca - 12 Basilica Giulia - 13 Tempio dei Dioscuri - 14 Tempio del Divo Giulio - 15 Chiesa di S. Maria Antiqua - 16 Tempio rotondo di Vesta - 17 Casa delle Vestali - 18 Regia - 19 Tempio di Antonino e Faustina - 20 Chiesa di S. Lorenzo in Miranda - 21 Tempio rotondo di Romolo - 22 Basilica di Massenzio o di Costantino - 23 Antiquarium del Foro - 24 Chiesa di S. Francesca Romana - 25 Tempio di Venere e Roma - 26 Arco di Tito.

IL PALATINO: 27 Giardini Farnesiani - 28 Casa di Livia - 29 Casa di Augusto - 30 Tempio di Apollo - 31 Domus Tiberiana - 32 Museo Palatino - 33 Palazzo dei Flavi - 34 Domus Augustana - 35 Stadio di Domiziano.

FORI IMPERIALI: 36 Foro di Cesare - 37 Foro Traiano - 38 Colonna Traiana - 39 Mercati Traianei - 40 Foro di Augusto - 41 Tempio di Marte Ultore 42 Foro di Nerva - 43 Foro di Vespasiano - 44 Mappe geografiche su marmo dell'Impero Romano.

LA VALLE DEL COLOSSEO: 45 Il Colosseo o Anfiteatro Flavio - 46 Arco di Costantino - 47 Meta Sudans - 48 Domus Aurea.

deutsch

FORUM ROMANUM: 1 Basilika Aemilia - 2 Kurie - 3 Kirche der Hl. Martina und Lukas - 4 Lapis Niger - 5 Septimius Severus Bogen - 6 Rostra - 7 Tabularium - 9 Tempel de Vespasian - 10 Saturntempel - 11 Phokas Säule - 12 Basilika Julia - 13 Tempel der Dioskuren - 14 Tempel des Julius Caesar - 15 Kirche der Hl. Maria Antiqua - 16 Vestatempel - 17 Haus der Vestalinnen - 18 Regia - 19 Tempel von Antoninus und Faustina - 20 Kirche des Hl. Lorenzo in Miranda - 21 Rund Tempelchen des Romulus - 22 Basilika des Maxentius - 23 Antiquarium des Forum - 24 Kirche der Hl. Francesca Romana - 25 Tempel der Venus und Roma - 26 Triumphbogen des Titus.

PALATIN HÜGEL: 27 Farnesische Gärten - 28 Haus der Livia - 29 Haus des Augustus - 30 Tempel des Apollo - 31 Haus des Tiberio - 32 Palatin Museum - 33 Palast der Flavier - 34 Domus Augustana - 35 Stadion des Domitian.

KAISER FOREN: 36 Cäsar Forum - 37 Trajans Forum - 38 Trajanssäule - 39 Märkte des Trajan - 40 Augustus Forum - 41 Tempel des Mars Ultor - 42 Forum des Nerva - 43 Forum Vespasians - 44 Karte des Romische Reiches.

VAL DES COLOSSEUM: 45 Das Colosseum - Amphitheater der Flavier - 46 Konstantinsbogen - 47 Meta Sudans - 48 Domus Aurea.

français

FORUM ROMAIN: 1 Basilique Emilienne - 2 Curie - 3 Église des Saints-Martine-et-Luc - 4 Lapis Niger - 5 Arc de Septime Sévère - 6 Rostra - 7 Tabularium - 8 Portique des Dieux Consentants - 9 Temple de Vespasien - 10 Temple de Saturne - 11 Colonne de Foca - 12 Basilique Julia - 13 Temple de Castor et Pollux - 14 Temple de Divi Jules César - 15 Église de Ste-Marie-Antiqua - 16 Temple de Vesta - 17 Maison des Vierges Vestales - 18 Regia - 19 Temple d'Antonin et Faustine - 20 Église de St.-Laurent-en-Mirand - 21 Temple rond de Romulus - 22 Basilique de Maxence - 23 Antiquarium du Forum - 24 Église de Sainte-Françoise-Romaine - 25 Temple de Vénus et de Rome - 26 Arc de Titus.

LE PALATIN: 27 Jardins des Farnèse - 28 Maison de Livia - 29 Maison d'Auguste - 30 Temple d'Apollon - 31 Maison de Tibère - 32 Musée du Palatin - 33 Palais des Flaviens - 34 Domus Augustana - 35 Stade de Domitien.

FORUMS IMPÉRIAUX: 36 Forum de Jules César - 37 Forum de Trajan - 38 Colonne de Trajan - 39 Marchés de Trajan - 40 Forum d'Auguste - 41 Temple de Mars Vengeur - 42 Forum de Nerva - 43 Forum de Vespasianus - 44 Cartes geographiques de l'Empire Romain.

LA VALÉE DU COLISÉE: 45 Le Colisée ou Amphithéâtre Flavien - 46 Arc de Triomphe de Constantin - 47 Meta Sudans - 48 Domus Aurea (Maison dorée).

español

FORUM ROMANUM: 1 Basílica Emilia - 2 Curia - 3 Iglesia de los Santos Martina y Lucas - 4 Lapis Niger - 5 Arco de Septimio Severo - 6 Rostra - 7 Tabularium - 8 Pórtico de los dioses Consentes - 9 Templo de Vespasiano - 10 Templo de Saturno - 11 Columna Foca - 12 Basílica Julia - 13 Templo de Cástor y Polux - 14 Templo de Julio César - 15 Iglesia de Santa María Antigua - 16 Templo de Vesta - 17 Casa de las Vestales - 18 Regia - 19 Templo de Antonino y Faustina - 20 Iglesia de San Lorenzo en Miranda - 21 Templeto circular de Rómulo - 22 Basílica de Majencio - 23 Antiquarium del Forum - 24 Iglesia de Santa Francisca Romana - 25 Templo de Venus y Roma - 26 Arco de Tito

EL PALATINO: 27 Jardines de la familia Farnese - 28 Casa de Livia - 29 Casa de Augusto - 30 Templo de Apolo - 31 Domus Tiberiana - 32 Museo del Palatino - 33 Palacio de los Flavios - 34 Domus Augustana - 35 Estadio de Domiciano.

FOROS IMPERIALES: 36 Foro de Julio César - 37 Foro de Trajano - 38 Columna Trajana - 39 Mercados de Trajano - 40 Foro de Augusto - 41 Templo de Marte Ultor - 42 Foro de Nerva - 43 Foro de Vespasiano - 44 Mapas geográficos en mármol de la Roma Antigua.

EL VALLE DEL COLISEO: 45 El Coliseo o Anfiteatro Flavio - 46 Arco de Constantino - 47 Meta Sudans - 48 Domus Aurea.

Estratto dal Poster ROMA ANTIQUA - Plastico della Roma Imperiale, Museo della Civiltà Romana.

POSTER OF THE IMPERIAL ROME
POSTER DELLA ROMA IMPERIALE

ENGLISH: 1. TEMPLE OF TRAJAN 2. ULPIAN BASILICA 3. MARKETS OF TRAJAN 4. FORUM OF TRAJAN 5. TEMPLE OF JUPITER MAXIMUS 6. THEATRE OF MARCELLUS 7. TEMPLE OF MARS ULTORES 8. FORUM OF AUGUSTUS 9. ROMAN FORUM 10. TEMPLE OF SATURN 11. FORUM OF NERVA 12. FORUM OF PEACE 13 BASILICA AEMILIA 14. TEMPLE OF ANTONINUS AND FAUSTINA 15. BASILICA JULIA 16. TEMPLE OF GOD AUGUSTUS 17. BASILICA OF MAXENTIUS 18. TEMPLE OF VENUS AND ROME 19. STATUE OF NERO'S COLOSSUS 20. BATHS OF TITO 21. BATHS OF TRAJAN 22. COLOSSEUM (THE FLAVIAN AMPHITHEATRE) 23. ARCH OF CONSTANTINE 24. TEMPLE OF THE CAESARS 25. DOMUS FLAVIA 26. TEMPLE OF APOLLO 27. HIPPODROME OF DOMIZIANO 28. PALATINE 29. DOMUS AUGUSTANA 30. CIRCUS MAXIMUS 31. TEMPLE OF CLAUDIUS 32. THE AQUEDUCT CLAUDIUS 33. PALACE OF SEPTIMIUS SEVERUS

ITALIANO: 1. TEMPIO DI TRAIANO 2. BASILICA ULPIA 3. MERCATI TRAIANEI 4. FORO DI TRAIANO 5. TEMPIO DI GIOVE MASSIMO 6. TEATRO DI MARCELLO 7. TEMPIO DI MARTE ULTORE 8. FORO DI AUGUSTO 9. FORO ROMANO 10. TEMPIO DI SATURNO 11. FORO DI NERVA 12. FORO DELLA PACE 13. BASILICA EMILIA 14. TEMPIO DI ANTONINO E FAUSTINA 15. BASILICA GIULIA 16. TEMPIO DEL DIVO AUGUSTO 17. BASILICA DI MASSENZIO 18. TEMPIO DI VENERE E ROMA 19. STATUA DEL COLOSSO DI NERONE 20. TERME DI TITO 21. TERME DI TRAIANO 22. COLOSSEO (ANFITEATRO FLAVIO) 23. ARCO DI COSTANTINO 24. TEMPIO DEI CESARI 25. DOMUS FLAVIA 26. TEMPIO DI APOLLO 27. IPPODROMO DI DOMIZIANO 28. PALATINO 29. DOMUS AUGUSTANA 30. CIRCO MASSIMO 31. TEMPIO DI CLAUDIO 32. ACQUEDOTTO CLAUDIO 33. PALAZZO DI SETTIMIO SEVERO

DEUTSCH: 1. TEMPEL DES TRAJAN 2. BASILIKA ULPIA 3.TRAJANSMARKT 4. FORUM DES TRAJAN 5. TEMPEL DES JUPITER MAXIMUS 6. MARCELLUS-THEATER 7. TEMPEL DES MARS ULTOR 8. FORUM DES AUGUSTUS 9. DAS ROMISCHE FORUM 10. TEMPEL DES SATURNS 11. FORUM DES NERVA 12. FRIEDENSFORUM 13. BASILIKA AEMILIA 14. TEMPEL VON ANTONINUS UND FAUSTINA 15. BASILIKA JULIA 16. DIVI AUGUSTI TEMPEL 17. BASILIKA DES MAXENTIUS 18. TEMPEL DER VENUS UND ROM 19. KOLOSSALSTATUE DES NERO 20. THERMEN DES TITO 21. THERMEN DES TRAJAN 22. COLOSSEUM 23. CONSTANTINSBOGEN 24. TEMPEL DER CÄSAREN 25. HAUS DER FLAVIER 26. APOLLOTEMPEL 27. PFERDERENNBAHN DES DOMIZIANO 28. PALATINHÜGEL 29. HAUS DES AUGUSTUS 30. CIRCUS MAXIMUS 31. TEMPEL DES CLAUDIUS 32. WASSERLEITUNG DES CLAUDIUS 33. PALAST DES SEPTIMIUS SEVERUS.

FRANÇAIS: 1. TEMPLE DE TRAJAN 2. BASILIQUE ULPIA 3. MARCHÉS DE TRAJAN 4. FORUM DE TRAJAN 5. TEMPLE DE JUPITER MAXIME 6. THÉATRE DE MARCELLUS 7. TEMPLE DE MARS VENGEUR 8. FORUM D'AUGUSTE 9. FORUM ROMAIN 10. TEMPLE DE SATURNE 11. FORUM DE NERVA 12. FORUM DE LA PAIX 13. BASILIQUE EMILIE 14. TEMPLE D'ANTONIN ET FAUSTINE 15. BASILIQUE JULIA 16. TEMPLE DE DIVI AUGUSTI 17. BASILIQUE DE MAXENCE 18. TEMPLE DE VÉNUS ET ROME 19. STATUE COLOSSALE DE NÉRON 20. THERMES DE TITUS 21. THERMES DE TRAJAN 22. LE COLISÉE (AMPHITHÉATRE FLAVIEN) 23. ARC DE CONSTANTIN 24. TEMPLE DES CÉSARS 25. PALAIS DES FLAVIENS 26. TEMPLE D'APOLLON 27. HIPPODROME DE DOMITIEN 28. LE PALATIN 29. MAISON D'AUGUSTE 30. CIRQUE MAXIME 31. TEMPLE DE CLAUDIUS 32. AQUEDUC CLAUDIUS 33. PALAIS DE SEPTIME SÉVÈRE.

ESPAÑOL: 1.TEMPLO DE TRAJANO 2. BASÍLICA ULPIA 3. MERCADOS TRAJANEOS 4. FORO TRAJANO 5. TEMPLO DE JÚPITER MÁXIMO 6. TEATRO MARCELO 7. TEMPLO DE MARTE ULTOR (VENGADOR) 8. FORO DE AUGUSTO 9. FORO ROMANO 10. TEMPLO DE SATURNO 11. FORO DE NERVA 12. FORO DE LA PAZ 13. BASÍLICA EMILIA 14. TEMPLO DE ANTONINO Y FAUSTINA 15. BASÍLICA JULIA 16. TEMPLO DEL DIOS AUGUSTO 17. BASÍLICA DE MAJENCIO 18. TEMPLO DE VENUS Y ROMA 19 ESTATUA DEL COLOSO DE NERÓN 20. TERMAS DE TITO 21. TERMAS DE TRAJANO 22. COLISEO (ANFITEATRO FLAVIO) 23. ARCO DE CONSTANTINO 24. TEMPLO DE LOS CESARES 25. DOMUS FLAVIA 26. TEMPLO DE APOLO 27. HIPÓDROMO DE DOMIZIANO 28. PALATINO 29. DOMUS AUGUSTANA 30. CIRCO MÁXIMO 31. TEMPLO DE CLAUDIO 32. ACUEDUCTO CLAUDIO 33. PALACIO DE SEPTIMIO SEVERO.

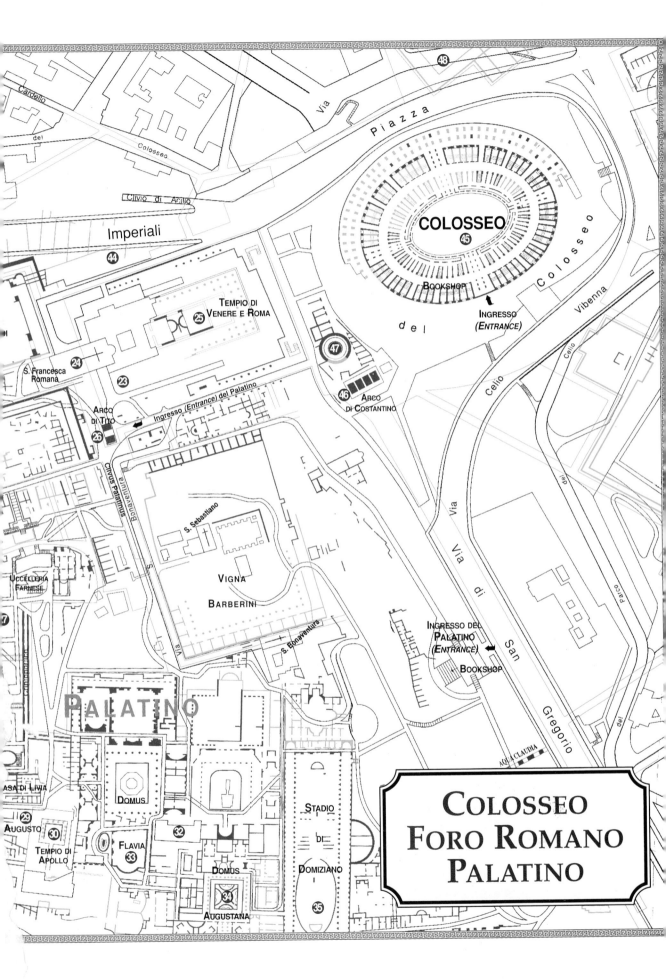

COLOSSEO
FORO ROMANO
PALATINO

MERCATI DI TRAIANO 39

38

37

FORO DI TRAIANO

MERCATI DI TRAIANO 39

40 FORO DI AUGUSTO

41

FORI IMPERIALI

42 FORO DI NERVA

43

Alessandrina

Via

dei

Fori

L.go Romolo e Remo

FORO DELLA PACE

FORO DI CESARE 36

Clivio Argentario

Via d. Tulliano

Via della Curia

Via della Salara Vecchia

INGRESSO DEL
FORO ROMANO (*ENTRANCE*)

BOOKSHOP

22
BASILICA
MASSENZIO
COSTANTI

SS. Cosma e
Damiano

20 (S. Lorenzo in
Miranda)

S. Maria
in Aracoeli

SC. dell'Arce
Capitolina

CURIA

3

CARCERE
MAMERTINO

Via d. Pietro in Carcere

Via dell'Arco di Settimio

BASILICA EMILIA 1

2

5

4

ROSTRA

11

TEMPIO DI
ANTONINO E
19 FAUSTINA

21

Sacra

Via

FORO ROMANO

14

18

Museo
Capitolino

Piazza
del Campidoglio

Palazzo
Senatorio

7 TABULARIUM

TEMPIO DELLA CONCORDIA

ARCO DI
SETTIMIO
SEVERO

6

9

Capitolinus

8

10 TEMPIO DI SATURNO

Via del Campidoglio

BASILICA GIULIA 12

13 TEMPIO DEI
DIOSCURI

16

17 CASA DELLE VESTALI

15

Via di Monte Tarpeo

Clivus

Via di Monte Tarpeo

di Giove

Via del Tempio

TEMPIO
DI GIOVE
CAPITOLINO

Via del Foro Romano

Via dei Foraggi

S. Maria
della Consolazione

Via d. Consolazione

P.za d.
Consolazione

Via dei

Via Bucimazza

SAN TEODORO

Via di S. Teodoro

Clivus

Vicus

ORTI
FARNESIANI

DOMUS
TIBERIANA

23

CASA D

Via Caprino

Jugario

Via di Monte

Via